WOMEN'S
Factory Work in
WORLD WAR I

Gareth Griffiths

The women are splendid. Woman's part in the war; not the tender nursing part – that was expected by all – but the great share she is taking in what was once man's work is one of the great surprises.... Women have successfully initiated themselves into new kinds of war work which had hitherto been regarded as coming only within man's sphere.

Lord Northcliffe, 1916

On the 11th hour of the 11th day of the 11th month the Armistice was announced. We were all stopped, just like that, no redundancy, nothing.

Female factory worker, Southampton, 1918 (Southampton Oral History Archive)

WOMEN'S
Factory Work in
WORLD WAR I

Gareth Griffiths

ALAN SUTTON

First published in the United Kingdom in 1991 by
Alan Sutton Publishing Ltd · Phoenix Mill · Far Thrupp · Stroud · Gloucestershire

First published in the United States of America in 1991 by
Alan Sutton Publishing Inc. · Wolfeboro Falls · NH 03896–0848

British Library Cataloguing in Publication Data
Griffiths, Gareth *1953–*
    Women's factory work in World War I.
    1. Great Britain. Factories. Women personnel. Social
    conditions, history
    I. Title
    331.40941

ISBN 0–86299–795–X

Library of Congress Cataloging in Publication Data applied for

Typeset in 11/14 Baskerville.
Typesetting and origination by
Alan Sutton Publishing Limited.
Printed in Great Britain by
The Bath Press, Bath, Avon.

For Anne Lineen

CONTENTS

ACKNOWLEDGEMENTS

This book could not have been produced without the generous help of many people and institutions: I am very grateful for the support given by the Health and Safety Executive library staff who made available the majority of the photographs in this book. In particular, I would like to thank Richard Lewis, Jill Gregory and Kate McNicholl for their help and interest. The staff of the Imperial War Museum were invaluable in helping me compare the photographs of the two archives and in tracing the background to the Women's War Work Committee. In addition I have received help and advice from Elizabeth Roberts of Lancaster University, Deidre Beddoe of the Polytechnic of Wales, Southampton City Museums Oral History Project, Manchester Studies Unit, Falkirk Museums, National Sound Archive and Leicester Oral History Archive. I am indebted to Sue Brook who typed up the manuscript so efficiently and to many friends who discussed the archive and its background with me, in particular Geoff Marsh and Mark O'Neil. Finally I must thank Anne Lineen who put up with me while I researched and wrote this book and to whom it is dedicated.

The overwhelming majority of the photographs in this book are from the archive held by the Home Office Industrial Museum produced by the work of the Women's Factory Inspectorate with the Women's War Work Committee. These photographs are now in the care of the Health and Safety Inspectorate. The photographs on pages 14, 34, and 62 are from the Falkirk Museum.

If any readers can supply any further information on the people in the photographs, or if their families have memories of factory work in World War I, I should be grateful if they would contact me by letter via Alan Sutton Publishing.

INTRODUCTION

The record of the impact of the 1914–18 war and the contribution of those involved is an uneven one both between the classes and the sexes. The major impact was of course felt by the non-commissioned soldier, although the popular image, derived from the record produced by the officer class, would have us believe that the officer class was one which suffered disproportionate losses. However, out of seven hundred thousand British losses in the war, thirty-seven thousand were officers. The literate drawn from the officer class have kept their memory fiercely alive through their poetry, novels, diaries, etc. The impact of the war on the women and their contribution to it was, however, largely unrecorded until in 1917 a movement grew to create a memorial to those involved with the war, a memorial in the form of a museum whose purpose was summarized as being:

> to collect and preserve for public inspection objects illustrating the British share in the war. The Exhibition will comprise examples of the arms and other war materials used by the British naval and military forces, trophies captured from the enemy, souvenirs found on battlefields, inventions connected with munition making at home, the literature and art of the war (including regimental magazines and trench drawings), maps, the music of the war, placards issued by the Government in connexion with the recruiting, economy and war campaigns, medals and decorations, flag-day souvenirs, and autographed letters of some of those who have taken distinguished parts in the war.

Out of this movement grew the foundation of the Imperial War Museum and a committee for recording the contribution of women to the war effort. The majority of the photographs in this book come from the archive produced by this initiative. In March 1917 the decision to create a National War Museum was announced and a committee formed with Sir Martin Conway as director general to oversee the collection of material and the acquisition of a site for the museum. Conway outlined the purpose of the museum:

> When peace returns and men are back at home, the years will pass and memory of the great days and adventures through which they lived grow dim. It's the purpose of the Museum to be a place which they can visit with their comrades,

Packing rope for the Navy in canvas

their friends, or their children, and there remember the past and behold again the great guns and other weapons with which they fought, the uniforms they wore, pictures or models of the ships and trenches and dug-outs in which weary hours were spent, or positions which they carried and ground every yard of it memorable to them.

The collection of material was delegated to four subcommittees which covered the three services and the fourth, 'The Women's Work Subcommittee', covered the contribution of women to the war effort, both at home and at the front. The Women's Work Subcommittee was chaired by Lady Norman and included Lady Haig and Lady Askwith with Conway's daughter Agnes as secretary. In the first months of its work the Women's Work Subcommittee confined itself to collecting material from secondary sources such as newspapers etc. Contracts were agreed between the subcommittee and the leading press agencies for copies of photographs of women who had received recognition for their contribution to the war effort, usually in the areas of voluntary service and nursing. Initially, the aims of the subcommittee were limited to collecting portraits of all women who had been either decorated, died in the service of their country or had performed outstanding deeds of valour. Most of this material was collected through newspapers.

Towards the end of 1917 a significant shift in the approach of the committee occurred. The appalling losses at Passchendale forced the proposals for the museum to be reviewed by a committee under Lord Crawford, one of whose members, the President of the Board of Education, H.A.L. Fisher, urged that the museum be more selective and not exhaustive. At this period the Women's Work Subcommittee was strengthened by the addition of two new members: Frances Durham, Chief Women Inspector of Employment at the Board of Trade, who later became Assistant Secretary in the Ministry of Labour, and Adelaide Anderson, the Chief Lady Inspector of Factories at the Home Office. These two women quickly began to organize the committee into adopting a more vigorous approach to recording women's contribution to the war effort. Working with Professor Chapman of the Board of Trade Statistical Department, Frances Durham submitted a scheme to collect the statistics of the employment of women. By the

Women conveying the crushed silica stone to the mill, South Wales, 1918

beginning of 1918 this statistical evidence was used by Durham and Anderson to tabulate the level of substitution of men by women in nineteen industries. From this statistical base the desire grew to create a photographic record of the 'significant' areas of substitution. By March 1918 the subcommittee was able to report that:

> In co-operation with the Chief Lady Inspector of Factories the Women's Work Sub-Committee is at work on the formation of a series of photographs for record purposes which shall show the most important processes in which women have acted as a substitute for men in the factories since the war.

On 20 August 1918 two photographers from the Department of Information were seconded to the Women's Work Subcommittee: H. Nicholls and G.P. Lewis.

Horace Nicholls had been employed by the Department of Information as their

Women washing the insides of the steel-ingot moulds before use, National Projectile Factory, 1918

official photographer on the home front since 1917. The photographs taken by Nicholls were not intended for use by the British press; instead they formed a part of the Department of Information's propaganda campaign abroad – which was at this period largely directed towards America. Nicholls had made his name as a photojournalist during the Boer War and on his return had specialized in photographing the Edwardian era. Lewis was unquestionably a very fine photographer although unfortunately very little else is known as he appears and then disappears almost without trace.

As soon as the two men were seconded to them in August, Durham and Anderson drawing upon the statistical archive they had built up, quickly organized the recording of women's work. Nicholls worked principally around London while Lewis covered the industries outside the capital. Lewis's visits to factories were organized through the Women's Factory Inspectorate; he was always accompanied by the local inspector who briefed him on the processes to be photographed. Particular attention was paid to producing a record of all aspects of working in a factory and many photographs were clearly taken to illustrate points of health and

Building rubber treads for motor tyres

safety. Lewis in particular managed to produce some strikingly 'natural' photographs which very effectively record the dirty and heavy work undertaken by the women. The range of industries covered by this ambitious project in a short period of time is astonishing: in one trip lasting a fortnight Lewis recorded women's work involving chemicals, flour, rubber, asbestos, glucose, india rubber, aluminium, paint, dye and munitions. In less than four months Lewis took over thirteen hundred photographs. By October 1918 enough material had been produced to enable the Women's Work Subcommittee to hold an exhibition of women's work at Whitechapel Art Gallery. The success of the exhibition, which quickly attracted eighty-two thousand visitors, reflected the extent to which, due to domestic press censorship, the nation knew as little about the work being carried out by women in the shipyards and engineering shops as they did about what was happening in the trenches.

At the end of 1918 Lewis left the project and the committee reviewed their progress in producing a record of women's contribution to the war effort. An obvious gap was the work of women in France which, with the cessation of hostilities, the committee was eager to record. Although Horace Nicholls was still working for the subcommittee it is interesting that they chose to appoint a woman, Olive Edis, to carry out the work. A recognized studio portraitist before the war, Olive Edis was at work for the subcommittee by March 1919 photographing the women working in France for the Red Cross, YWCA and the Voluntary Aid Detachment. Edis brought a new depth to the project record:

> Edis was photographing something new, not only to her in terms of photographic practice, but also to the women who were her subjects. Their excitement and energy emerges clearly in the many portraits which Edis produced . . . her war workers have a grace and presence which speaks of their confidence as skilled and informed women . . . the central theme of her work is a documentary of busy accomplished women.

The post-war world did not bring the bright future that women workers and women inspectors had hoped for. Women workers faced disappointment and unemployment as the new avenues that had opened up during the war were closed to them once again. The women factory inspectors struggled with issues such as the place of women in the work-force of a peace-time economy; in the first two weeks after the armistice one hundred and thirteen thousand women were discharged. Adelaide Anderson observed, 'too little thought seems to have been given, by those discharging women, to what might be done in the way of adaptation of work for them or improvisation of training to prevent their unemployment.' By 1920 Anderson's annual report made grim reading, not only had women been shut out of 'mess' industries, but males had replaced females in some industries that had once been considered the province of women. Even in laundries, methods were changed to create jobs for disabled soldiers, and many of the skilled jobs women had done were eliminated. The frustrations of women who were removed from their wartime jobs were summarized by a factory inspector:

> During the war, women's powers and capacities were called into full play and no one denies that there was a response beyond all exception. Today there is little call to a strenuous and sustained effort, entailing full use of powers and faculties. Instead, interesting work is taken out of their hands, and they are being forced back into the routine of their hitherto normal occupations. (Factory Inspectorate Report 1919)

On the completion of Olive Edis's work in France in 1919 the Women's War Work Subcommittee was disbanded. The archive was divided between the new photographic department of the Imperial War Museum and the Home Office's Factory Department. The Home Office's collection later passed to the new Home Office Industrial Museum in 1927.

In 1978 the doors closed on the Home Office Industrial Museum which was established to 'promote the safety, health and welfare of industrial workers'. The Home Office Industrial Museum was opened on 3 December 1927, becoming the Safety, Health and Welfare Museum in 1946, in Horseferry Road, Westminster. As early as 1910 the concept of a museum which would demonstrate the latest techniques of safety and welfare was approved by the Treasury, based upon similar museums in Milan, Berlin, Munich, Amsterdam, Paris and Lausanne which had been in existence since the beginning of the century under the name of 'Workmen's Welfare Museums'. The new museum, which incorporated the latest safety features in its design, was completed by 1914 when World War I delayed it's opening. Influential in creating a movement for the foundation of the museum was the *Daily News* 'Sweated Industries Exhibition' held in the Queen's Hall, London in 1906. Among the key organizers of the exhibition were Mary MacArthur of the Women's Trade Union League and Margaret Macdonald of the Women's Industrial Council who were closely involved with the Women's Factory Inspectorate.

When the museum opened, it had a floor space of around ten thousand square feet in which the approved techniques for protecting the industrial worker against accidents were demonstrated, together with examples of conditions to promote the health and welfare of the work-force. The museum was run by an inspector from the engineering section of the factory inspectorate, with an emphasis placed upon working exhibits. The safety features included within the building's design were the latest examples of modern lighting, heating and ventilation as well as new features such as non-slip treads and a vacuum cleaning plant. It was intended that the museum would be used by trade unions, manufacturing associations, medical and technical colleges, as well as the designers of factories, machinery and power plants, and the manufacturers of machinery guards and other protective appliances. The factory inspectorate also used the museum as a training centre where the principles of industrial safety were taught; within the museum there was a cinema and a lecture theatre. The awesome task of the museum was to make an impression upon the visitor of the terrible level of industrial injuries; the scale of this task is indicated by the following comparison:

World War I 1914–18	*British Industry 1919–24*
British wounded 1,693,262	Industrial injuries 2,385,766
	(killed 20,263)

The museum was divided into three sections: the first covered the latest techniques for safeguarding workers using power machinery in industries ranging from shipbuilding and the textile industry to woodworking and the chemical industry; the second covered labour-saving devices, rescue apparatus and industrial diseases, as well as welfare – canteens, recreation, first aid and protective clothing; the third reviewed examples of ventilation, lighting and heating, as well as noise insulation and the clothing to be worn by workers in dangerous or dirty occupations. The museum displayed both good and bad practices, which included equipment that had caused injury: a grim exhibit was a torn mass of rags, just recognizable as being the clothes of a man dragged into machinery when his clothing was caught in an unprotected revolving shaft.

Of great interest was the photographic collection and film archive held by the museum; many of the photographs were taken by factory inspectors recording a wide range of working conditions. At the core of the archive was the important collection of photographs taken during World War I to record the contribution of women to the war effort. The creation of this archive is inextricably linked to the development of a Women's Factory Inspectorate and the movement in the late nineteenth century to collate information on the domestic and working conditions of the working classes as a tool to influence legislation.

The Women's Factory Inspectorate

Since 1833 male factory inspectors had enforced the factory laws. In 1842 the law forbidding the employment of women underground in mines was passed, followed by the Ten Hours Act which limited the workday of women and children in the textile industry. The Ten Hours Act was extended in 1867 to cover all factories employing more than fifty people. Many organizations concerned with women's welfare and rights feared that the protective legislation would result in unemployment for women; which indeed it did in many industries. Initially, the Women's Provident and Protective League (later to become the Women's Trade Union League) opposed the protective legislation arguing that it would severely restrict job opportunities for women. Following the 1847 Act however, the League decided that if the protective legislation was to be of any use to women, women had to be involved in the inspection of factories. Following a long campaign, the first 'Lady Factory Inspector', May Abraham, was appointed in 1893 together with Mary Muirhead Paterson. May Abraham had been secretary to Emilia Dilke, the leader of the Women's Trade Union League. The success of these appointments was such that a year later two more inspectors were appointed: Lucy Deane and Adelaide Anderson.

The work of the factory inspectorate was by no means limited to the inspection and correction of conditions in the industrial workplace; of equal importance was the collection of data to support the amendment of existing rules and to assist the passage of new legislation. It is clear that the women inspectors supported the view that the collection of statistics was an essential part of the approach to improving the conditions of working women; this philosophy is echoed by the founding resolution of the Women's Industrial Council which had close links with the founding members of the factory inspectorate:

> In the opinion of this conference it is desirable that a central council shall be established to organise special and systematic inquiry into the conditions of working women, to provide accurate information concerning those interests, and to promote such action as may seem conductive to their improvement.

To achieve this end the council would 'investigate the actual facts of women's work, and collect and publish trustworthy information about the conditions of their employment.'

This interest in social issues dates to the 1840s. The passion for quantification derived from methodically-classified facts, on the surface the most rational and ordered means of social investigation, grew. This is exemplified in the growth of statistics as a science: the Board of Trade set up a statistical office in 1832, the British Association founded a statistical section in 1833, and in the same year Manchester and London both founded statistical societies.

Charles Booth's *Life and Labour of the People in London*, the first volume of which was published in 1889, opened an era of statistical social research which grew out of

Booth's desire to 'create a large statistical framework which is built to receive accumulations of facts out of which is at last evolved the theory and the law and the basis of more intelligent action.' The Women's Factory Inspectorate had close links with this movement for social investigation. May Abraham worked on the Royal Commission of Labour 1891–4 with Clara Collet who had previously worked with Charles Booth as an investigator into the conditions of women's work in the East End. Beatrice Potter (Webb) worked closely with Booth in the early stages of his survey and was a friend of Abraham as were Gertrude Tuckwell, Margaret Llewellyn-Davies and Ben Tillet. Seebohm Rowntree, who carried out his own survey in York following Booth's London survey, worked closely during World War I with the Women's Factory Inspectorate on women's welfare in industry. A further link between the late nineteenth-century social survey movement and the women's factory inspectorate is provided by Sir Hubert Llewellyn Smith who later became the director of the committee that undertook the 'New Survey of London Life and Labour' in 1928, and was a contemporary of Rowntree. Llewellyn Smith was a member of Booth's team of investigators and he later joined the Board of Trade and the Ministry of Labour, where he worked closely with the Women's Factory Inspectorate during World War I analysing the degree to which women were replacing men in industry.

World War I

The immediate effect of the outbreak of war was a drastic increase in unemployment, and many of the industries worst hit were those which, in peacetime, employed large numbers of women. In dressmaking, only 34 per cent of women workers were working full-time; in boots and shoes a mere 13 per cent of women workers were in full-time employment. To mitigate this position a Central Committee on Women's Employment under Mary MacArthur was established to organize relief work. The Central Committee was advised by the chief lady inspector of factories, Adelaide Anderson, and the local committees were supported by the district factory inspectors. Soon, however, there was a shortage of skilled labour as the war created a demand in industries which traditionally employed women. 'Substitution', the extensive use of women in place of men in industry, began on a limited scale in the summer of 1915. With the introduction of conscription for men in January 1916 women increasingly replaced men throughout industry. During the war the number of women employed in industry increased by over a million, with approximately 700,000 replacing men. For

Steel shell bars being cut by circular saws. Note the absence of protection for the hands or face

example, in July 1914, 212,000 women were employed in metal and engineering industries; by July 1917, 819,000 were employed.

As the demand to meet production quotas grew it became unpatriotic to talk about limiting hours of work or be too demanding about safety. The Home Office permitted the relaxation of the Factory Acts. Shift work, long hours, Sunday work and shorter mealtimes all became the norm. Sylvia Pankhurst took up the matter of the long hours and poor conditions that women worked under:

> Sometimes a woman wrote to me, broken down in health by overwork, complaining of long walks over sodden, impromptu tracks, ankle deep in mud, to newly-erected factories; of night shifts spent without even the possibility of getting a drink of water; of workers obliged to take their meals amidst the dust and fumes of the workshop. (*The Home Front* 1932)

Concern about the conditions of work for women led the Ministry of Munitions to establish a commission to 'consider and advise on questions of industrial fatigue,

A basic mess room in a munitions factory, 1918

hours of labour, and other matters affecting the personal health and physical efficiency of workers in munition factories and workshops.' Working with Seebohm Rowntree who was a member of the commission, the women inspectors supplied Rowntree with 1,396 surveys of conditions in factories which employed nearly two hundred thousand women. The results were classified 'according to the degree of urgency for his attention': 31 per cent of the factories were rated as acceptable; 49 per cent of the remaining factories were rated as second class; and 20 per cent were rated as third class as they lacked adequate meal rooms, washing and first-aid facilities, rest rooms, and 'suitable supervision'.

During World War I as the numbers of women employed in industry increased so the number in domestic service declined. As may be expected, industries connected with munitions saw the most dramatic increase, most notably the metal and engineering industries. The growth of women's employment in different industries during the war is shown by the table below:

Employment of Women in Industry 1914–18

Trade	Estimated number of women employed			% of females in work force	
	July 1914	*July 1918*	*Difference*	*1914*	*1918*
Metals	170,000	594,000	+424,000	9	25
Chemical	40,000	104,000	+ 64,000	20	39
Textile	863,000	827,000	− 36,000	58	67
Clothing	612,000	563,000	− 44,000	68	76
Food/Drink	196,000	235,000	+ 39,000	35	49
Paper/Printing	147,000	141,000	− 6,000	36	48
Wood	44,000	79,000	+ 35,000	15	32
China/Earthenware	32,000				
Leather	23,000	197,000	+ 93,000	4	10
Other	49,000				
Government Establishments	2,000	225,000	+223,000	3	47
TOTAL:	2,178,600	2,970,000	+792,000	36	37

(Taken from the Report of the War Cabinet Committee on Women in Industry 1919)

At the time of the outbreak of World War I the nature of women's employment was already changing. New opportunities for women in the fields of clerical, shop and factory work offered higher wages and shorter and more regular hours than those enjoyed by women employed as domestic servants, which was by far the major occupation for women until World War I. Until 1914 the total number of domestic servants was still growing, although at a slackening rate compared with the closing decades of the nineteenth century. During World War I the proportion of women in factory work rose rapidly with the introduction of conscription for men in 1916. By the end of the war the number of women munitions workers had

Grinding bases of grenades, Castlelaurie
Foundry, Falkirk Iron Company, 1917

risen from 212,000 to 900,000, while the number of female domestic servants had
fallen from 1,658,000 to 1,250,000. After the war there was, according to a
government report, a reluctance in women to enter domestic service. The report
noted: 'amongst girls a growing distaste to enter domestic service under its present
conditions, and a reluctance on the part of parents to allow them to take up such
work.' As domestic service declined in popularity among younger women, so the
age of those employed in service rose. In 1891, 40 per cent of those employed in
service were below twenty; by the outbreak of World War II over 50 per cent were
aged between thirty-five and fifty-five.

Percentage of working women employed as domestic servants, 1881–1931:

Year	Percentage in domestic service
1881	44
1901	40
1911	34.5
1931	24

During the period 1914–18 there were broadly three stages in the development of women's employment in industry:

i) The expansion of women's work within trades which were traditionally major employers of women: textiles and clothing.

ii) The substitution of women in many male occupations to release men for the forces.

iii) The concentration of women in government munitions factories, frequently newly-built factories.

With the outbreak of war, the immediate effect upon women's employment was to create unemployment on a widespread scale, particularly in industries associated with women:

At the beginning of the war a London firm of theatrical costumiers in a large way of business wrote to ask if I could help them to find some work which would enable them to keep their staff of nearly 200 women employed. Orders in their own trade had entirely failed owing to there being no new productions at the theatres, and pantomime orders being cancelled. I advised them where to apply, and eventually they secured a War Office contract for khaki uniforms and a sub-contract for shirts, and the empty workrooms were once more in full work. The same weekly wages were paid as when the workers were on theatrical costumes, but the firm were content for the time being to make no profit rather than that their staff should be disbanded and the factory closed down.

The furriers were found to be suffering severely at the outbreak of the war; the early autumn would, normally, find all this industry busy preparing the winter goods: ladies' muffs and neckwear, fur coats and linings for men and ladies' wear. But on the day after the declaration of war orders from wholesale houses were cancelled and the retailers' demand ceased. Relief came to this trade early in October with the placing of orders from the War Office for fur and skin coats for the troops. Immediately all furriers were fully occupied, and a shortage of fur sewers and machinists became a serious difficulty in the execution of the contract. (Women's factory inspector 1915)

The Women's Factory Inspectorate noted that 'the phase of unemployment and short time, following immediately on the sudden alarm and shock of war, was felt throughout our industries and by almost all workers to some degree, but most intensely of all and for the longest time by women.'

Towards the end of 1914 some industries expanded rapidly as they received orders to supply the forces:

Women trimming stockings and gloves

the large trades involving women, in which there was an incessant, increasing demand for their labour, are:- woollen and worsted textiles (khaki, flannel, blankets); hosiery clothing (military tailoring and fur coat making, cap making, shirt making); boots and shoes and other leather articles . . . surgical dressing and bandages, tin canister and box making.

. . . Miss Taylor, a factory inspector whose district includes the important clothing trade in Leeds, reports that the pressure of work consequent on the demand for uniforms has precipitated a change which has slowly been taking place throughout the year, that is the gradual conversion of workshops into factories. During the last three months of the year the demand for soldiers' and sailors' clothing has exceeded the amount the combined forces of the trade can supply. At the same time the demand for civilians' clothing was very small. The nature of the khaki work makes it impossible for places equipped only with treadle machines to turn it out at remunerative prices. Therefore, unless they are to be continually out of work it becomes necessary to fit power to their machines. April and May have hitherto been the months when the notification of new factories was heaviest. The notifications for the last six weeks have been exactly double what they were in April and May. Since the beginning of the war 45 new clothing factories have been added to the registers on a total of 420. Whether this increase is likely to be permanent it is impossible to say. One of the most important industries in which occupiers in Glasgow and other districts have adapted themselves to new conditions is that of carpet making, some of the looms in several carpet factories having been successfully adapted to the weaving of Army blankets. Another instance of industrial development was in a canvas bag factory where a number of women, girls and men have, since the outbreak of war, been employed in the making of nosebags for horses, engaged in sewing the bottoms to the bags. In two factories, in one of which hosiery is manufactured and in the other Army uniforms, additional British labour being unavailable, the management have taken on a few Belgian women and girls. (Factory Inspectors Report 1915)

The demands of the war economy did not necessarily bring improvements in conditions of employment or wages for women. The *Women's Dreadnought* throughout 1914 published allegations that women working for government contractors were working at sweated rates of pay:

Jameson's of Poplar, Government contractors, pay women 2s. 1d. a dozen for making soldiers' shirts. One woman who has been making boys' shirts for 2s. 6d. a dozen, to be sold to private firms, tells us that she refused Government work until there was no more private work to do. She tells us that the soldiers' shirts, besides being paid at lower rates, are larger and more complicated than others, and are of harsh stuff that makes the women's fingers sore. The shirts are dark and the cotton black, and the work therefore tries the eyes a good deal. The women can only manage to do a dozen shirts a day, by working very hard and out of the 2s. 1d. they earn by this, they have to pay 2½d. a reel for cotton – a reel does not do quite a dozen shirts ... strange patriotism this, that allows the Government contractors who are making money out of this war to sweat the women workers in this disgraceful fashion.

In March 1915 the government took steps to create a register of women who were willing to undertake war work. The response was immediate and within six months over one hundred and ten thousand women had registered. However, prejudice

Forming the patterns on jacquard cards for lace production

against the employment of women restricted the numbers of women who were found employment through the register to five thousand. This deeply ingrained prejudice against the employment of women outside their traditional areas of work was only broken in late 1915 when the shortage of munitions forced the government to establish a Ministry of Munitions which encouraged the employ-ment of women in the munitions factories which were declared 'controlled establishments' and so fell outside trade union restrictive practices. Employment in the munitions factories was generally better paid than most industries, and as women moved away from their traditional areas of employment into the better paid munitions work a shortage of labour was created in the clothing and textile industries towards the end of 1915. The shortage of women in textiles became so acute that some Lancashire textile manufacturers asked that the school leaving age be reduced to twelve. The reorganization of munitions production by the Ministry of Munitions, which could legally enforce the suspension of trade union practices, paved the way for the large-scale mobilization of women into other industries. Dilution officers were appointed to increase and encourage the dilution of male labour in factories. The dilution officer visited factories in order to assess the amount of labour required and how production could be met by using female labour wherever possible. A further impetus to the use of women was given in January 1916 when conscription for single men was introduced and was followed in May by the introduction of universal conscription. The rapid use of women is indicated by the employment of over half a million new women workers in munitions work between July 1915 and July 1916. Munitions work became far more popular among women than the traditional women's trades; the Women's Factory Inspectorate reported in 1915: 'The difficulty at present is in the replacement of women who have left the so called women's and lower paid industry to take a hand in work formerly done by men,' Large numbers of domestic servants grasped the opportunity to escape service, as was reported by *Domestic News*:

> With the coming of the war domestic workers in large numbers gave up their work for other occupations and it was not all patriotism that prompted them, rather a desire to escape a condition of employment that was distasteful to them on account . . . of what may be termed the bondage of domestic service.

Women painting aeroplanes by means of the aerograph, a mechanical paint-spraying machine, Austin Motor Works, Northfield, near Birmingham

The overwhelming majority of the women working in industry were working class; Monica Cosens, a middle-class volunteer for munitions work, estimated that only 9 per cent of munitions workers were middle class. Her memories of work in a munitions factory convey a sense of isolation: 'Frankly I did not like the look of my companions. They were rough, loud voiced and gave me the impression of being ill natured and having sharp tongues.'

The explosion of employment in munitions during 1916 and 1917 was paralleled by the substitution of men by women in other industries. Increasingly women replaced men in industries such as chemicals, building, metalworking, food and drink, and the ship and aircraft industries. By 1917 the *Labour Gazette* was estimating that a third of working women were replacing male workers. The trade unions saw women as a threat to their wage rates and pre-war conditions of employment. Initially, the unions attempted to restrict the areas of employment for women. However, when the process of substitution could no longer be resisted, they argued that women should be paid the same rates as men in order to prevent them undercutting the men's rates. This gave rise to the Treasury Agreement which was a contract between the government and the unions, whereby the

Pottery kiln being loaded prior to firing,
Stoke-on-Trent, 1918

conditions of substituting men for women were agreed. The unions were promised that skilled men's rates would be maintained and that women replacing them would receive the full rate. In addition, agreement was reached that after the war, pre-war conditions should return to the industries and the agreements would not lead to any permanent substitution of men by women and the semi-skilled or female labour would be the first discharged when hostilities ceased.

Although a range of agreements was made on the use of women throughout the war, opposition to women being employed in industries previously dominated by men continued and took many forms. A woman tool fitter reported several instances of harrassment by her fellow male workers: 'My drawer was nailed up by the men, and oil was poured over everything through a crack another night.' While another woman who worked in an engineering works recalled: 'I was sacked. There was a man who chewed tobacco and kept spitting in my pocket and I hit him'. There is little doubt that the women had to contend with:

> the strong feeling, largely shared by the employer and the male workers, that they had no business to be in the factories at all. Their failures therefore produced a far greater psychological impression than their successes; and failures which were the fault of management or of the skilled supervision were readily attributed to them.

Throughout the war there was concern over what the effects of industrial employment upon the women would be. Reports ranged from the transformation of once strong and healthy women into 'pale and anaemic creatures with no vitality and no joy in living' to patriotic descriptions of women whose hard work 'does not seem to be doing much harm to their health for their eyes are bright, their cheeks are fresh and there is hardly any evidence of fatigue among them.'

Reviewing the effect of wartime employment upon women the War Cabinet Committee's Report on Women in Industry reported that they considered that women's health had actually improved during the war due to improved health care, nutrition and physical work. In her evidence to the War Cabinet Committee Dr Janet Campbell submitted that an improvement in the standards of women's health had occurred during the war years. Prior to the war, malnutrition had been one of the main causes of ill-health, anaemia and stunted physique among women. Campbell's observations were supported by Mary MacArthur who maintained that before the war:

> women are more liable to incapacity by sickness than men and it is my contention that (apart from normal physical reasons) this extra sickness in women is due to their greater poverty and to the character of their employment.

Long hours, long standing, lack of fresh air, long intervals without food, are undeniably, especially in the case of young anaemic girls, detrimental to health and the low wages which attach to most women's employment involve insufficient and often improper food.

Dr Mary Deacon of the National Amatol Factory in Liverpool reported that in her experience of looking over seven thousand women and one thousand men she found that 'men could not work longer, though they could do heavier work . . . women had a higher standard of factory hygiene than men.' She found 'no grounds that women grew more fatigued than men and so had more accidents. Women who worked at night could not get proper sleep at daytime and this contributed to minor ailments. No gynaecological trouble was caused by women working in factories.' (War Cabinet Committee 1919)

Working in munitions factories and other industries did involve risks to the health of the workers who handled chemicals such as TNT. Women working with explosives developed such symptoms as coughing, swellings, burns and eruptions on the skin. During the first two years of the war, inexperience of the dangers of working with TNT led to over a hundred fatalities from TNT poisoning as well as many serious illnesses. An investigation by the Home Office led to new sets of regulations on the safety and health of munitions workers which included clauses about cleanliness, ventilation, washing facilities, the provision of free milk, special uniforms and the appointment of full-time medical officers. Other industrial processes other than munitions involved hazards to health, for example, women working in foundries suffered from the fumes: 'We had to see a doctor once a month . . . because there were fumes and we had to wear masks. We were allowed a pint of milk a day . . . we used to have two hours up (in a crane) and two hours down, we had to rest, you see.' (Female foundry worker 1916–17)

Alongside the concern for the health of women working in industry was official alarm at the falling birth-rate creating a sense of urgency to establish an infant and child welfare system. The increased concern for infant welfare was expressed in a number of campaigns throughout the war, one of which was 'National Baby Week' held in July 1917. The week was opened by the Queen who was received by a guard of honour made up of 120 mothers and babies. Certainly the war did stimulate an interest in how child welfare services could be improved: in 1914 local authorities employed 600 health visitors and this had soared to 2,577 by 1918. Similarly the number of child welfare centres rose from 350 to 578 by 1918. Reviewing the creation of the School Medical Service the Chief Medical Officer to the Board of Education wryly noted:

The School Medical Service has emerged from the War . . . bearing not only evidences of the struggle, but also the complete vindication for its existence and of its recognition as the educational portion of a national system of Preventive Medicine. The returns of the medical examinations of recruits to HM Forces, and their import in connection with recruitment and the national physique, directed public attention to the findings and results of the School Medical Service, and drove home the lesson that the nation was suffering from its neglect to detect the earliest beginnings of disease, and to take steps to prevent as far as possible their development into physical disability. As a result of the War there has arisen a new conception of the value of the child to the nation.

Women v. Men

The wartime conditions provided an unexpected opportunity to test the assumptions about women's employment, by placing women in jobs previously held by men. Prior to the war it had been assumed that women could only perform certain kinds of work: light, sedentary, indoor work, especially labour which did

Women construction workers on the site of a new aircraft factory for Jolly's, Birmingham

not require a high degree of strength or skill, intellectual or physical. There was a consensus before 1914 that only the relative cheapness of women's labour offered any inducement to an employer to employ women in preference to men. The demands of industry during the war put these assumptions to the test. Following the war there were attempts to review the performance of women by various employer federations who found that overall their fears about the unsuitability of women for industrial employment were unfounded. In many areas women performed better than men, taking on jobs or occupations which normally required a term of apprenticeship which would exceed the period of the war. The ability of women to acquire skills considerably faster than the normal apprenticeship period had the effect of undermining the apprenticeship system, as Walter Greenwood in *Love on the Dole* (1933) noted:

> 'You're part of a graft, Harry;' he said: 'All Marlowe's want is cheap labour; the apprentice racket is one of their ways of getting it. Nobody teach you anything simply because there's so little to be learnt. You'll pick up all you require by asking questions and watching others work . . . . Your apprenticeship's a swindle, Harry. The men they turn out think they're engineers same as they do at all the other places, but they're only machine minders. Don't you remember the women in the war?'
>
> 'What women?' Harry asked, troubled by what Larry had said.
>
> 'The women who took the places of the engineers who'd all served their time. The women picked up straight away what Marlowe's and other say it takes seven years' apprenticeship to learn.'

In addition to having to learn their skills quickly, outside the normal apprenticeship scheme, women had to combat the reluctance on the part of skilled men to teach women:

> In every industrial district without exception, there was continuous opposition to the introduction of women. In some cases this opposition was overt to the point of striking; in other instances . . . it took the insidious form of refusal to instruct women, or attempt to restrict the scope of their work or to discredit their efforts. (Home Office Report 1919)

These and other disadvantages were to some degree counterbalanced by the introduction of new labour-saving devices and machines during the war.

The substitution of men by women led to a series of agreements between the government and the trade unions defining under what conditions substituted

A man and a woman working together in the saw-milling industry

labour could be taken on. These agreements formed the basis of the Treasury Agreement of March 1915 and were implemented by the Munitions of War Act 1915. The agreement between the government, employers associations and trade unions was broadly:

i)   The rate customarily paid for a job should not be lowered on the importation of a different type of labour (whether that of women, unskilled men or juveniles).

ii) That the suspension of restrictions on such other types of labour 'hold good only for the duration of the war, or till such time as sufficient male labour should be again available.'

The attitude of the trade unions towards the employment of women, in part dictated by men's ideas as to what work it was 'proper and decent' for women to

Fixing the nose clips to gas masks, Holloway Road, London

perform, had also been influenced by the fear of the effect of women's competition in ousting men from occupations or in lowering their standards of life.

The quality and value of the contribution of women was summarized by the Home Office after the war:

> The opinion of the Factory Department is recorded that the substitution (of women for men in industry during the war) has proved successful in a great majority of cases; that women have shown capacity to take up many of the more skilled processes hitherto reserved for men and to carry them out completely and well, and have displayed unexpected readiness for work which at first sight seemed wholly unsuitable for them. (War Cabinet Committee 1919)

Commenting upon the division of duties and work which had occurred before the war the report further noted:

> Occupations with demarcation between men's and women's work or duties . . . cover the bulk of the occupations in industry proper. Though often the lines of

demarcation are artificial, it is rarely that they do not exist . . . . There are many cases where women's work in one district or factory, is men's in another district or factory.

Collecting evidence on the quality of the work performed by women, the Home Office received submissions from most industries including the Federation of Master Printers who, in a number of cases, paid women less than men although their output was higher. The employers gave as a reason for this inequality, that the women's output might then fall as low as the men's if their pay was increased! The type of labour in which women were found to be more valuable workers than men was light work of a repetitive nature, or work requiring special dexterity – often work classed as men's work before 1914. There were skilled processes which had been considered definitely and exclusively men's work before the war at which women became rapidly expert:

In some skilled trades, such as acetylene welding, where the process, reserved before the war to fully-skilled fitters, boilermakers or coppersmiths, was more or less specialised, the women did 'interchange' jobs with the men and it was pretty generally accepted that woman's output is equal to the man's . . . in some cases it is said to be better. (Factory Inspectorate Report 1920)

The medical officers, working in industry, noted the changes in women with their increased role in industry:

Most women enjoyed the more interesting, active and arduous occupations, and in many cases their health improved rather than deteriorated. Medical officers of factories and welfare supervisors have pointed out the beneficial effects of open-air conditions (yard work, trucking of raw materials etc.) on the general health, and the success with which properly selected women have undertaken work involving the lifting of weights, heavy machine work, and even forge and foundry work, without untoward physical consequences. The whole experience tends to show that light sedentary work is not by any means always the most suitable for women. That operations involving a change of posture are preferable and that given an adequate nutrition many women would have better health and greater physical vigour if they followed more active occupations . . . . The conditions under which women were employed before the war were not such as to enable them to develop full health and vigour. Low wages, and unsatisfactory and inadequate diet, long hours and lack of exercise in the open air, resulted in physical and industrial inefficiency and caused both men and women to place too low a value upon the woman's strength and capacity. The results of employment of women under war conditions have emphasised the importance to health of good food, clothing and domestic comfort which can be obtained when the wages represent a reasonably adequate recompense for labour. They have also proved that properly nourished women have a much greater reserve of energy than they usually had been credited with and that under suitable conditions they can properly and advantageously be employed upon more occupations than has been considered desirable in the past even when these involve considerable activity, physical strain, exposure to weather etc. Light sedentary occupations are not necessarily healthy occupations. (War Cabinet Committee on Women in Industry 1919)

The conclusions of the War Cabinet Committee on Women in Industry (1919) were that, before the war, women had been paid such low wages that they could not feed or support themselves properly; and this had set up a vicious circle of low wages, low efficiency, and low valuation of their work. Examining the effects of employment in industry and the health of women and their children, the War Cabinet Committee came to the following conclusion: 'Employment under suitable conditions is not itself injurious to the pregnant woman, while the money thus earned may enable her to be properly fed, a matter of the highest importance.'

During the wartime period, there were low infant mortality rates, when an increasing number of mothers were being employed in industry. Clearly irritated by the persistent search for differences between men's and women's ability to carry out industrial occupations Dr Butler, the medical officer of the Scottish Shell Filling Factory at Paisley, told the War Cabinet Committee:

There has been a tendency to exaggerate the physiological differences between men and women which is mainly connected with women's maternity function. Generally speaking the health of women who had worked indoors – domestic service etc., improved considerably with good food and physical work. . . . there is no industrial work as heavy as charing and women should not be prevented from doing any work they are fit for, including foundry work, heavy engineering and heavy chemical work.

The report of the 1919 War Cabinet Committee assessed the contribution of women to the war effort and examined the future role of women in industry. The committee collected a wide range of evidence relating to women's work, both before and during the war. However, in producing its findings and recommendations the committee was constrained by two fundamental assumptions: that men had a prior right to paid employment, and that the performance of domestic tasks was a function inseparable from womanhood. The committee recommended that a national minimum wage for women should be laid down by law, based upon the subsistence needs of a single woman; a pensions scheme was also advocated for women who had to support children without the aid of a man. The committee unanimously agreed that:

> No woman should be employed for less than a reasonable subsistence wage – that this wage should be sufficient to provide a single woman over eighteen years of age in a typical district where the cost of living is low, with an adequate diet, with lodging to include fuel and light in a respectable house not more than half an hour's journey, including tram or train from the place of work, with clothing sufficient for warmth, cleanliness and decent appearance, with money for fares, insurance, Trade Union Subscription and with a reasonable sum for holidays and amusements.

The effect of these proposals was practically nil; no legislative provision was made for a national wage for women, and widows received a pension seven years after the proposals were made. Only Beatrice Webb, a member of the committee, raised a voice in opposition to the report attacking the assumption 'that industry is normally a function of the male, and that women . . . are only permitted to work for wages under special conditions.' Beatrice Webb's proposals, arising out of the experience of women working in industry during the period of World War I are of great significance particularly when one considers how relatively recently some of the proposals have been encompassed in legislation. Her five main proposals were:

i) That there should be a national minimum wage, which should be equal for men and women.
ii) That there should be standard rates of remuneration for every occupation, which should be equal for men and women.
iii) That the principle of the 'vested interest' or prior right of the male to any occupation should be rejected.
iv) That provision should be made for children by the State.
v) That adult dependants (such as aged, infirm and sick) should be also provided for as a national obligation, 'because it is not desirable that one adult should be dependent upon another adult for maintenance.'
(Report of War Cabinet Committee, Minority Report 1919)

Reviewing the year following the end of the war, R.E. Graves, the Chief Inspector of Factories, felt that British industry had adjusted well to peacetime production and accommodating the demobilized men:

The first year after the cessation of hostilities has been a very notable one for industry, and it is remarkable how complete has been the change over from war to civil production, and with what wonderful smoothness this stupendous task has been accomplished on the whole. The first great step in the transformation was the gradual, and now almost complete, withdrawal of women from the men's industries where they performed such magnificent service during the War, and the absorption into industry of the demobilised men. (Women's Inspectorate Report 1919)

One of the lady factory inspectors added:

The change back has been effected with far less effort than was the earlier change from civil to war production, and this is largely an effect of the careful substitution agreements of employers and workers made in so many industries under the guidance of the Factory Department. (1919)

The difficulty for many men and women was that while acknowledging that the enormous expansion in the size of the women's work-force had led to far-reaching economic and social changes, they found enormous difficulty in upholding the rights of both men and women to employment and equality of pay. The president of the Women's Labour League Congress in 1917 spelt out the dilemma facing women when the men returned from the front:

After the war . . . was the woman going back like Joan of Arc to her plough and rough menial work? After delivering her country and laying down her armour was she going to leave the arena of commerce to lay down her uniform and go back to her pots and kettles, to unpaid and unconsidered labour or to the lower alleys of factory work?

Certainly the women themselves wished to remain in employment; in answer to the question posed in 1916 – 'Do you wish after the war to return to your former work or stay in what you are doing now?' of the 3000 answers, 2500 were 'To stay in the work I am doing now.' It was clear that women did not want to return to their traditional and ill-paid jobs of the pre-war period. During their wartime employment women had gained substantially by achieving regular, well-paid employment, which allowed them and their families a higher standard of nutrition and health. However, even more important than their increased spending power was their greater freedom and importance in society and their acknowledged role within it. This feeling of a greater role within society was summarized in a letter to the *Glasgow Herald* in 1916:

Work more traditionally associated with women: girls finishing teddy bears in a toy factory, Nell Foy, Church Street, Chelsea

To observe how men speak and write about women today is vastly amusing to us. We have not changed with the war; it is only that in some instances the scales have fallen from men's eyes . . . . In the hour of Britain's need her sons have realised that if victory was to be won they could not afford to hem women in with the old restrictions. To carry on the industries of the country women must work . . . . A few years ago I heard Lord Charles Beresford say 'A woman's place was her home'. Twelve months ago I heard him say 'Woman's place was in the world'.

In spite of wishing to remain in their wartime industries, the demobilization of troops forced women out of their jobs and back into their 'traditional pre-war areas of work' with their associated low pay and poor conditions. The pressure to leave their jobs was enormous, campaigns were run in the press to 'persuade' women where their work lay:

Women still have not brought themselves to realise that factory work, with the money paid for it during the war, will not be possible again . . . . Women who left domestic service to enter the factory are now required to return to the pots and pans. (*Southampton Times* 1919)

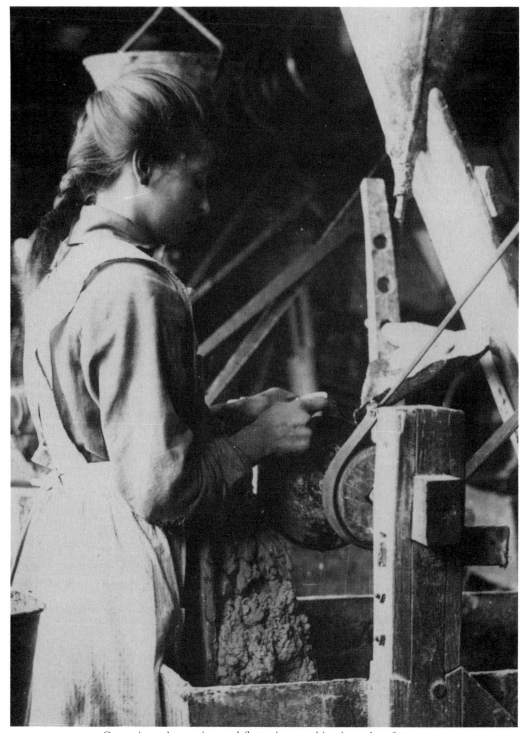

Operating a bottoming and flattening machine in a glass factory

Photographs from

THE WOMEN'S WAR WORK COMMITTEE

———

Milling 6-in chemical shells, Castlelaurie Foundry, Falkirk Iron Company

WOMEN'S WELFARE AND WORKING CONDITIONS

Throughout the period of the war considerable concern was expressed by organizations concerned with the welfare of women, of the effects of eight hundred thousand women entering industrial employment. The Women's Factory Inspectorate paid particular attention to the ability or inability of previously male-dominated industries to adapt to the employment of large numbers of women. Details were noted on the provision of medical and dental care, cloakroom arrangements, baths and washing arrangements, the provision of overalls, waterproofs, gloves etc., workroom cleanliness, seating accommodation and messroom arrangements.

In many industries men and women were working together for the first time; concern was expressed over the safety of the women, night work raising particular difficulties. In general, unmarried women were not normally encouraged to carry out night-shift work. In most factories night-shift work was carried out under the supervision of a female supervisor and in ammunition factories a nurse was on duty should tiredness result in fainting. Women factory inspectors urged the provision of a good meal during the night shift. In some factories the organization of meal breaks could be complicated; at one factory women were escorted to and from the dining-room, and when the women's shift left the factory a police patrol was on duty. Where the women workers could not be segregated from male workers concern was frequently expressed:

In Birmingham factories the manufacture does not lend itself to a division between men's and women's work or to the employment of girls under a forewoman. Men and girls work side by side in big sheds filled by machinery. The sheds are situated in large yards which often at night are insufficiently lighted, and undoubtedly the women workers are exposed to serious risk. (Factory Inspectorate Report 1917)

At the outbreak of the war the great majority of factories and workshops lacked any proper provision of messrooms or canteens; a survey in Sheffield at the start of the war showed that only 30 per cent of the factories provided simple dining rooms or areas where the work-force could eat their food. The introduction of night shifts for women, together with the difficulty for many women of obtaining food during the day due to rationing, led to improved conditions for canteens and messrooms; the Home Office in granting orders for night work expressly laid down the condition that suitable provision had to be made for messroom facilities. In many cases dining rooms and small kitchens were built; most new factories had facilities where workers could heat and eat a meal away from the factory floor. An inspector commenting upon the need for adequate catering noted:

How greatly the army of industrial workers need a commissariat department to cater for them during their days of active service will perhaps be better realised now that the public attention has been riveted on the victualling of our soldiers in camp and at the front. If 'an army fights on its stomach' is it not also true that a factory works on it? On the one hand the workers require the opportunity to buy good nourishing food and to eat it under good conditions, on the other the money to spend on a sufficient dinner – to illustrate these needs the following out of numerous examples are given. A large factory has since the war been filled to its utmost capacity, working long hours on uniforms – at a dinner hour visit I found in every room on six floors, 12 rooms in all, the workers were seated at their work-tables and sewing machines eating their mid-day meal. The stuffy rooms were for the time a restaurant, the smell of cooked vegetables and fish being added to the general smell of humanity and cloth. The manager was much concerned, and asked if nothing could be done; he said he had spoken about it to his Directors till he was tired and there was no available room for a mess-room, and the restaurants and eating-houses in the neighbourhood were overfull in the dinner hour already. The workers were making good wages on War Office contracts, the Factory Act secured them the hour's break, they were hungry, the Army needed all the work these girls could turn out at top speed, but for lack of opportunity unsuitable and insufficient food was eaten under the very worst conditions. Referring to the second point, that sufficient money to spend on food is required, is illustrated by the fact that at a large East End restaurant where the mid-day meal is served daily to a hundred workers from a neighbouring factory the Superintendent and her helpers had for years deplored the insufficiency of the dinner purchased by the young girls under 16. Meat and vegetables were purchased by the elder girls and women, but a little pudding and gravy or tea and bread and butter was all the younger ones could afford. The ladies felt that these needed it as much as their elders, and could scarcely refrain from supplying more than was paid for. One day soon after war broke out there was such a run on meat and vegetable dinners that the supply was not equal that day to the demand – all the young girls were asking to be served with them. The cause was that the wages had that day been raised voluntarily by the occupier to the proposed Trade Board rate, and the effect was immediate, and has continued. This fact is a striking answer to those who cling to the theory that an increase in wages is of no substantial value to a girl. (1916)

In an attempt to encourage their work-force to take part in outdoor activities when away from the work-place, some firms provided allotments, sports fields and activity rooms. When the women's factory inspectorate came across such provision they often described them with a sense of amazement:

Two firms have erected large buildings: they have billiard rooms, smoking rooms, rest rooms and restaurants all under the same roof. Clubs for sports as well as gardening; dramatic societies are organised and special teachers are appointed to teach gymnasium. A firm in the country near Bristol provides a certain number of allotments on which the workpeople can grow their own vegetables etc. This cannot be done in London, but one firm in the East have done their best to encourage workers who are keen on gardening and they have a club which provides seeds and gives information as to the best way of growing different plants, and award prizes for the best results that can be obtained in the East End backyards and window-boxes.

I saw a novelty in swimming baths at one factory where the entire roof is covered with two water tanks, one for boys and one for girls.

Despite such improvements, the inspectors came across frequent instances of the most appalling working conditions for women. Adequate sanitation was frequently a problem:

In the potteries where, in the past, considerable effort was made to get the local authorities of the Five Towns to give this matter their attention, great strides have been made during last year in altering and re-building sanitary accommodation. We have sent to the County Borough of Stoke over 100 notices of insufficient, insanitary or unsuitable accommodation for women. The Chief Inspector of Nuisances has kindly sent me a return of the work done during the year in his Borough, which shows that out of 1,413 defects found 1,294 have been remedied. Miss Whitlock reports that foul smelling privies are still met with and sometimes the number of conveniences is very inadequate, e.g., one convenience was found in one case for over 70 women. A small charge to workers for the cleaning of closets is fairly common, but the general standard of cleanliness in these places is not high. Miss Escreet found better conditions in Leicestershire than those to which she was accustomed in Lancashire but considers the metal trades and brick works of Staffordshire behind even the low standard of Lancashire.

In one town notices had to be sent in the case of 36 factories out of the 54 visited, and represented elementary defects in sanitation and suitability. Several bad cases have not yet been remedied though the original visits were paid in April and May.

Accommodation in brick yards is of the poorest. Notices of instruction to firms were sent in respect of 17 of the 22 works visited and further attention will be given to the matter in the current year. As the industry is a country one, the conveniences are privies, and careful scavenging arrangements should be made: these are frequently badly neglected. The women's and men's conveniences often stand doorless or unscreened side by side in a deserted portion of the yard, being totally unprovided with artificial light. It is amazing that such conditions should have been allowed to persist so long.

The problems of ventilation, excessive temperatures and poor lighting exercised the factory inspectors considerably. The textile and clothing industries together with the laundry industry raised particular problems in these areas:

In the large clothing factories, where power is readily available, the need for a more efficient and scientific system of ventilation remains obvious. Some occupiers still appear to have a rooted belief that a really good sized fan, revolving at the rate of many hundred revolutions a minute is a panacea for all the evils in connection with the vitiated air of factories. Repeatedly an occupier has taken us to see his fan, and has asked us to watch its revolutions and to calculate for ourselves the number of cubic feet of air and the number of microbes which the fan is hustling out of the factory each moment of the working day, and then it has been necessary to point out that the fan is so placed that it only creates a 'short circuit' and a draught in its own immediate neighbourhood. I hope that by the continued taking of air samples we may create a radical change in the present often defective installations. In some of the large factory laundries the need of more efficient means of ventilation, and of reduction of temperature raised by the steam and gas-heated machines is still pronounced. A factory which may be recorded as regular at one visit may, on another occasion, be far from healthy owing to atmospheric conditions. As Miss Ahrons points out, the ventilation of the town laundry is a difficult matter. Surrounded on all sides by factories and buildings with chimneys emitting smoke and dirt and filling the air with impurities, the windows and ventilators are often shut to prevent the smuts falling on the work. The occupiers complain that the fans draw the dust in through the various openings, so not only does the close proximity of the buildings shut out the fresh air, but the available means of ventilation are not sufficiently used. In one very enclosed laundry a propulsion system of ventilation by means of fans and ducts had recently been installed, but these ducts were laid near the floor, and the ventilating openings were covered with wire screens to prevent the entrance of dust and dirt. Although expense had been incurred by the installation of this plant very little benefit so far seemed to have been derived.

With women replacing men in many industries which involved labouring particular concern was expressed on the effect of the work on the physical health of the women. Before the war, women were involved in industries which required them to lift very considerable weights:

Owing to a complaint from a mother employed at an aerated water works that she considered the heavy work of lifting and carrying done by the women had been the cause of the still-birth of her baby, I made some enquiry in one factory. (a) Crates of twelve empty syphons weigh 68lbs.: they are lifted by a woman washer from the buffer's wheel to the washing machines. (b) A crate of 28 empty bottles (pint size) weight 42lbs.: such crates are lifted from the stack of cases of empty bottles a few feet off by a girl of 17 to the washing tank. (c) A crate of two dozen 10 oz. crown lemonade bottles weights 56lbs.: such crates are lifted by a woman from the bottling machines to the labeller's bench.

Also owing to a complaint as to the heavy nature of her employment, received from a young mother employed in a brick works, whose baby had died almost immediately after birth, and who returned to the factory within a month of her confinement, I visited the brick works at which she had been employed. I found that the women fill and empty the stoves in which the bricks are fired, that they take off at the making machine, also riddle and build up the bricks in the yard. Two women and two men form an emptying squad, the women being employed only in the kiln, while the man wheels away the brick laden bogie. A filling squad is composed of two women and one man, the man wheeling the bricks from the making machine, while the women build up the bricks. The weight of the largest brick is about 8¼lbs. The women lift two of these bricks simultaneously, one in each hand, both in filling and in emptying the kilns, and as the total number of bricks made averages 13,000 a day, each woman lifts about 6,500, i.e., over 52,000lbs. or 464cwt. The temperature in the warmest part of one of the kilns at a point at which the women were emptying, I found to be from 103°F., the outside temperature being 48°.

Following the war an assessment of women's ability to undertake heavy manual labour was carried out by a number of employers' federations; in general they found that one man's work might be replaced by 1.6 to 2.8 of a woman's, although with the introduction of labour-saving devices this ratio was considerably reduced in some industries.

In organizing the work of the two photographers, Nicholls and Lewis, the Women's Factory Inspectorate clearly used their local inspectors to brief the photographers fully on the industrial processes to be recorded and the details – such as the positioning of the hands near dangerous machinery, clothing, safety garments worn, etc. which they wanted recorded. These photographs were later then incorporated into the department's library of 'good and bad practice'.

One woman could vividly recall the terrible conditions she worked in after more than fifty years:

The outside of this grim establishment looked dark and dirty, the windows in the compressed leather department were boarded half way up, this I presume was to stop vandalism but it did nothing to improve the dark, damp smelly interior where about forty young girls and women toiled for ten hours every day clad in thick heavy shoes and a large heavy leather apron to protect their clothing which, by the way failed miserably, for one could not fail to correct some of the evil smelling concoction you worked with, from attaching itself to your blouse. It was a huge place, one side having heavy long tables at which each girl was allocated about four feet of working space, standing in close proximity of each other, but never daring to speak for fear you would hear your number called out, with the order to go home for the day and the words 'you have come here to work not to a party'. Despite this there were moments when the overlooker would leave her point of vantage and some daring mortal would burst into song, tho God knows what any of us had to sing about in these conditions.

The main heavy gates opened into a kind of archway and it was from this point the gatekeeper rang his bell, this being up in the belfry on the top of the buildings. It was rung every morning to signal us both in and out, if you were two minutes late after the clanging, which could be heard quite a considerable distance away, you were fined three checks or the equivalent of three pennies. This we could ill afford, and should the dreaded sound occur before we were near the gate we would run as fast as our legs could carry us to try to defeat its dreaded purpose. Once through the portals you were safe for the gatekeeper must lock them, this was one of his tasks. There was a glass-top-roof lean-to building which served as a cloakroom, dining room, at one end stood an old iron gas stove, no oven just open jets on the top which when covered with an iron plate was used for hotting the dinners we carried in our baskets from home, in a basin of course. For frying there was one iron frying pan which we took in turns to use as the occasion arose. We also took it in turns to light the stove and on Friday, after dinner, scrub the wooden tables we ate off, very rarely was the floor touched except for a quick sweeping and the walls of the place were festooned with spiders' webs, so much for the dining room. The toilets where intricacies I never did understand for they were only flushed about once a day by some unseen method. These also we took turns to clean, for the washing of our hands there was a huge tank filled from the River Leen whose waters were used in the process of tanning, no towel or even rag to dry them on, no such luxury. (Nottingham tannery worker 1917)

Woman stone worker sand-blasting a memorial stone wearing a protective hood and gloves

Sewing asbestos mattresses by hand for lining boilers on ships

Sheet of glass being carried out of the warehouse

Outdoor labourer working in a paper mill

Clean modern canteen room for munitions workers, 1918

An exemplary factory canteen dining-room

Small mess room for textile workers. Note the segregation from men and the presence of a woman supervisor

Modern canteen kitchen with warming stove to the fore and gas oven on the right, 1918

Simple rest room for foundry workers to rest in and eat their own food. 'First of all we worked full-time from six o'clock in the morning till five at night, and from five at night till six in the morning and that was the nights . . . as they got more girls in, they thought they would get more work out and they worked it at the eight hours . . . that was, six to two and two till ten and ten till six in the morning and that was the three shifts.' (Foundry worker 1918)

Clothing worn by flour millers

Outdoor protective clothing worn by a brewery yard worker

First-aid room in munitions factory

Rest room in a small factory

Washing facilities in a large textile factory

Woman doctor running a surgery for munitions workers. 'She hadn't a hat on and of course it was a drilling machine. They're easy enough to them drilling machines, you just drill a hole for the screw. Anyway she just happened to turn her head and her hair was loose and caught her hair in it. The screams, it was terrible, I remember it now.'
(Engineering factory worker)

Simple bathroom in a factory. This would have been regarded as being most rare at this period

Gymnasium for women

Athletics ground for textile workers

Allotment for factory workers

METAL INDUSTRIES, MUNITIONS AND OTHER WAR WORK

In the metal industries before World War I women were employed in tin-plate manufacture and wire drawing, as well as in the making of chains, nails, bolts, screws, rivets, etc. They were also employed in the production of light castings and allied trades (tinned and japanned goods). In the tin-plate industries they were employed in pickling and preparing the plates for the tin bath. In chain-making they made the smaller hand-hammered chains used mainly for agricultural purposes. Women fed the nail-cutting and tack machines, working in the Black Country and Birmingham on light machines for turning, screwing and pointing bolts, and for facing and topping nuts. Women were also employed in the warehouses, packing and bagging all these articles. Before World War I the machines were all set by male tool setters.

In general engineering women were employed before World War I mainly in specialized factories in the midlands on repetition work. They worked on capstan lathes, power hand presses, stamping, drilling, plating and hand soldering. The machines for the production of several components for small-arms ammunition in Birmingham and Newcastle were worked by women, although this was unusual for the period.

During World War I, it was first and foremost the requirements for munitions which brought women into the metal trades. Up to December 1914, only three thousand women had entered the industry. Over the following six months the shortage of munitions became increasingly acute. Initially, attempts were made to increase production using the existing male work-force by improving production techniques; women were gradually introduced during this period but were restricted to the unskilled processes. By the second half of 1915, the failure of the munitions industry to meet the demands of the war led to another 45,000 women being absorbed by the industry and the dilution process began in earnest, with women replacing men in many areas of production. Between July 1914 and July

1918 the numbers of women employed in the metal industries rose from 170,000 to 594,000, 90 per cent of whom performed work customarily performed by men. To the 424,000 women who entered the industry an additional 223,000 should be added as these were the women who worked in national establishments producing munitions, most of whom worked on metal. Unsurprisingly, the most important area of activity was shell making. By the middle of the war, women formed 60 per cent of the work-force producing shells and were involved with all aspects of shell making from the roughing and turning of the bodies to the final gauging of the completed shell.

> [My first job was] filling 9.2 gas shells . . . and they started us first on stemming the shells there was a certain amount of the powder measured out to you and you had to start on the shell from the bottom to the top and the stem was just like the handle of a brush, and of course you had a wooden mallet and then you had to start and hammer from the bottom to the top because you had to get it all in and if you didn't there was too much left over . . . . I was promoted from stemming shells to a press operator and of course we weren't allowed to wear any of our clothes, we had to strip out. If you had linen buttons on there was tin inside, you see and it would cause an explosion . . . we were supplied with cocoa going on duty and coming off and we had our own surgery and doctor . . . . The nurse examined us, they could tell by the colour of our eyes whether the gas was affecting us in any way. Your hair didn't go yellow but when you went to bed as you took your head off the pillow the pillowslip was pink. (A munitions worker in a gas shell factory)

In general engineering shops, shipyards, aircraft factories, etc. women were introduced to most varieties of men's work – light engineering, turning, shaping, machine riveting, crane-driving, soldering, welding; some women were promoted to the normally protected male areas of responsibility of fitting and turners. This process of introducing women to the engineering workshop was to greatly hasten the pre-war movement for specialization on the shop-floor and the subdivision of processes.

At the end of the war the National Employers' Federation submitted an assessment of the performance of women working in the engineering and metal industries in comparison with men. With regard to output it concluded:

1. *Quality:*

Sheet metal – Women's work better than men's output.
Engineering – Women's output equal to that of boys.
Repetitive light work – Women equal to men and boys.
Aircraft woodwork – Women equal to men in most areas.

Cartridge production – Women equal to men.
Shell production – Women's work poorer than men's.

2. *Quantity:*

Sheet metal – Women's production equal to 99 per cent of men's output.
Engineering – Women's production equal to 75 per cent of men's output.
Repetitive light work – Women's production equal to men's output.
Aircraft woodwork – Women's production equal to men's output.
Cartridge production – Women's production equal to men's output in some
    cases 20 per cent more than men's.
Shell production – Women's production behind that of men and boys.

For labouring tasks three women were considered as being equivalent to two
men and generally the Employers' Federation placed women's wartime production
as being two-thirds of men's in value. Overall, women equalled and sometimes
surpassed men's work, but could not compete for lack of training or physical
reasons – it was found that for light repetitive work women were both more
efficient and productive. Some employers suggested that women's production
involved more waste. However, a major employer in the midlands running six
shell-making factories testified to the waste produced by women as being
'infinitesimally low'.

Women were prohibited from being involved in the actual processes of smelting
throughout the war, but women performed the same work as boys in cold-rolling,
and to some extent in pickling and opening tin plates – a heavy operation. In many
factories women were employed as unskilled labourers performing heavy labouring
duties and as crane-drivers.

They took me up, showed me the controls – after a couple of days you got used to
it. . . . You had to come down every hour and a half to drink milk to get rid of the
effects of the fumes. You drank half a pint of milk to clear the fumes. (Female
crane operator, Southampton Oral History Archive)

Woman tin-plate worker feeding the cold rolling machine at the Beaufort Tin Plate Works, Maureston, South Wales in 1918

Tin plates about to be dipped into pickling baths at the Beaufort Tin Plate Works

Women trucking tin plates from the pickling room at the Beaufort Tin Plate Works

Woman tin-plate worker removing the tin plates from the annealing stand at Beaufort Tin Plate Works. Many women's hair turned white due to the acid fumes

Tin plates being separated. The work-bench is situated by the window to make the best use of natural light

Women munitions workers operating a circular saw to cut a steel bar in the production of shells, possibly at the National Projectile Factory, 1918

Women steel workers handling the hot slag heads into which the waste slag is poured, National Projectile Factory, 1918

6-in chemical shells being cleaned, Falkirk Iron Company, Castlelaurie Foundry, 1917

Women carrying 6-in chemical shell cores, Falkirk Iron Company, Castlelaurie Foundry, 1917

Women labourers emptying the ash wagons from the steelworks, National Projectile Factory, 1918

The inspection room of the foundry where the steel bars were inspected for quality, National Projectile Factory, 1918

Women operating lathes in the production of steel rails, David Brown & Sons, Sheffield, 1918

Women operating punching machine in foundry to produce 'fish plates' for the railways, David Brown & Sons, Sheffield, 1918

Woman crane driver moving a load of steel rails, David Brown & Sons, Sheffield, 1918

Women milling the calibration sections for range-finding equipment, Barr and Stroud, Glasgow

Women engraving and dividing the scales on range finders for the Navy and Army, Barr and Stroud, Glasgow, 1918

Women assembling the instrumentation for naval fire-control systems, Barr and Stroud, Glasgow

Making the rubber mouth pieces for the gas masks using moulds, Crowndale Works, Camden Town, London

Cleaning and examining the glasses for eye-pieces in gas masks, Crowndale Works, Camden Town, London

The oven room for producing splinterless glass for gas masks, Crowndale Works, Camden Town

Batches of gas-mask lenses being loaded into an oven for firing, Crowndale Works, Camden Town, London

The doping room at the Crowndale Works, Camden Town where the canvas masks were sealed against gas

Detail of the doping process for gas masks. Crowndale Works, Camden Town, London

Sewing of nose clips for gas masks, unknown factory in Holloway Road, London, 1918

The packing room, unknown factory in Holloway Road, London, 1918

WOOD AND AIRCRAFT TRADES

During World War I the proportion of women employed in the wood and aircraft trades increased from 15 per cent to over 33 per cent of the total work-force. Women were involved in wood-milling, sawing, planing, assembly, painting, polishing, varnishing, doping and metalwork. The work-force increased by thirty-five thousand women, twenty-three thousand of whom directly replaced men. A few thousand of these went into saw-milling but the turnover was high as the work was extremely heavy and required long training. The most important area was aircraft manufacture; at the outbreak of the war the industry was still in the experimental stage employing a small work-force of skilled mechanics and woodworkers such as cabinet-makers. By the end of the war the industry was composed of a series of subdivided processes where over a third of the work-force was female. By the end of 1918, fifty-five thousand aircraft had been produced.

Women were involved in the cutting and sewing of the linen fabric for the fuselage and wings, as well as painting on the acetate dope and assembling the aircraft. There was much resistance to the employment of women in any areas involving woodcutting and woodworking by the National Amalgamated Furnishing Trades Association. A circular, issued by the Minister of Munitions in 1916, which urged employers to take on female labour in the aircraft industry, met with so much opposition that it had to be withdrawn. Subsequently the National Aircraft Committee laid down that 'women should not be permitted to use edge tools' or to be employed 'on any wood-cutting processes connected with aircraft.' 'Substituted' women in aircraft woodworking were mainly employed in assembly work or in the cutting and sewing of linen fabric for the aircraft bodies.

Woman aircraft worker constructing the centre portion of a frame for an aircraft wing. 'My brother was working on aeroplanes, they were up and coming then, so I thought, why can't a girl go down there? They are taking girls to work on the sewing part of the wings. They were covered in linen and then doped (moisture proofed). That was done in a loft. They employed about ten or twelve girls.'
(Aircraft worker, Southampton)

Card splicing the joints on the frame of a wing for an aeroplane, Austin Motor Works, Northfield, near Birmingham

Taping and preparing the frames of the wings
in preparation for the canvas covering, Austin
Motor Works, Northfield, near Birmingham

Women stitching the canvas on the fuselage covers, Austin Motor Works, Northfield, near
Birmingham

Women doping the wings of an aeroplane, Austin Motor Works, Northfield, near Birmingham

The national markings being painted on the wings of an aeroplane, Austin Motor Works, Northfield, near Birmingham

Women metalworker acetylene welding frame lugs for plane assembly, Austin Motor Works, Northfield, near Birmingham

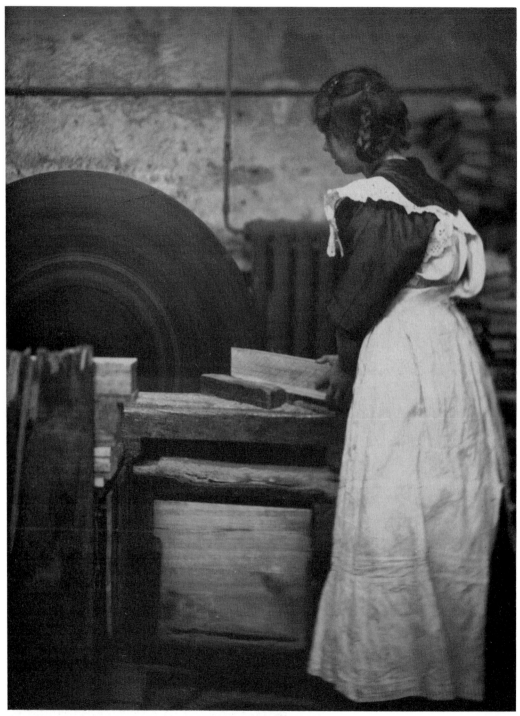

Young girl operating the circular saw at N.G. Tarrant and Sons. Note the absence of protection for the face and hands

Women 'trucking' the side-pieces for the production of ammunition boxes, N.G. Tarrant and Sons

Assembly of packing cases for ammunition, N.G. Tarrant and Sons, 1918

Woodworkers machine-wiring batches of side-pieces for ammunition boxes, N.G. Tarrant and Sons, 1918

CHINA AND EARTHENWARE TRADES

In 1914 two-fifths of the work-force were female in the china and earthenware industries, about 60 per cent of whom were employed in the Stoke-on-Trent district. Women were usually employed in departments on their own: working as decorators, aerographers, transferers, potters' attendants or dippers' helpers, as well as working as labourers in the yard and in the warehouse. In some areas of production women competed with men before the war: bowl-making, plate- and saucer-making and dipping. During the war the numbers of women increased by 10 per cent, some five thousand women directly replacing men.

Due to the dangers of lead poisoning, women involved with dipping or aerography were supposed to undergo a monthly medical throughout their period of war work. The women factory inspectors were alert to the dangers of lead-poisoning, cases of which were reported before the war:

> Poverty, with its attendant worry and lack of nourishment, appeared to be a predisposing cause in many cases ... in one case occurring in the first year of lead work, the patient had a gastric ulcer and in another case in the first year of lead work the patient had a stillborn child.

In these industries enormously heavy loads were carried by women. At the outbreak of war the inspectors found young women carrying wads of clay which weighed 48 lb. Worse cases were reported in the brickworks where an inspector found:

> the temperature at floor level to be 120°, 112°, and 108°, and girls under 18 were employed in filling and pushing barrows of bricks, 50 bricks at a time, weighing 425lbs. In this case the weight was not so trying as it might be as the barrow was one of four wheels and therefore easy to push. In other places the barrow is on three wheels and the girls lift by the handles instead of pushing so that the burden is far greater even though the actual weight is less – 306lbs. Miss Taylor says 'nine bricks weighing 8lbs., total over 60lbs., would be lifted as part of the work all day long. The foreman at one of these works said to me, 'There is no work so hard as this throughout the country,' and I am sure he is right. (Factory Inspectorate Annual Report 1913)

Bricks being loaded on to railway wagons by female yard workers, Hathern station, Brick and Terra
Cotta Company Limited, Leicestershire, 1918

Women yard workers feeding the machine for recovering silica stone, South Wales, 1918

Women brickmakers trucking clay from the mills for silica brick making, South Wales

Trucking clay to the moulding house, South Wales

Woman brickworker filling brick moulds with silica clay

Concrete bricks being pressed into moulds

Women silica brickworkers, South Wales, 1918

Women yard workers packing the dried concrete bricks in railway wagons

Woman yard worker emptying limestone slag from railway wagons

Women trucking limestone rocks

Women clinker house workers

Hoppers being filled with limestone

Bagging the cement

The quality of cement being tested by a laboratory worker

A granite block being positioned before being
sawn by machine

A polisher being adjusted above a block of granite

Woman worker, in a protective hood, sand-blasting a memorial stone

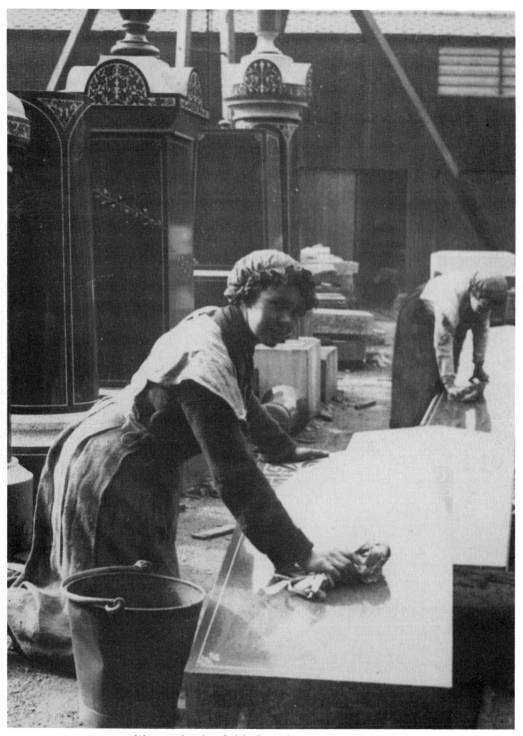

Women cleaning finished granite memorial stones

Draughtswoman

Used moulds being cleaned before reuse, Stoke-on-Trent, 1918

Fired taps being ground, Stoke-on-Trent, 1918

Fettling an absorption tower, Stoke-on-Trent, 1918

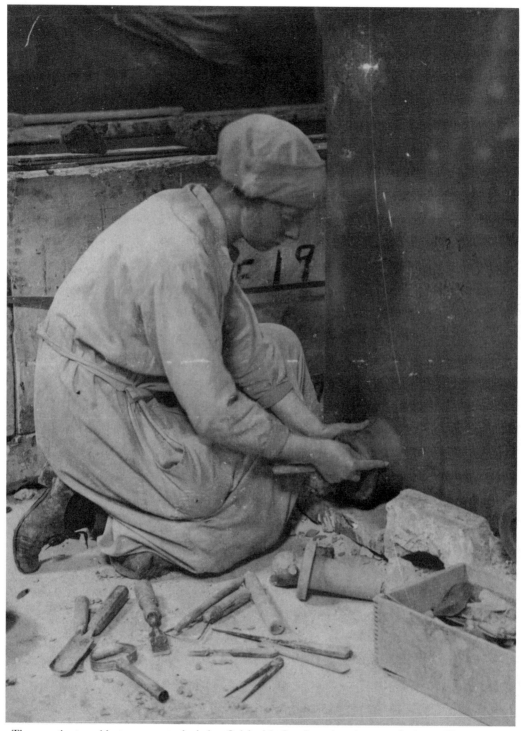

The mouths to acid stoneware tanks being finished before inserting the taps, Stoke-on-Trent, 1918

Preparing the plates for nitrating pans which were used in the manufacture of gun cotton, Terra Cotta Works, Leicestershire, 1918

Moulding and finishing plates for nitrating pans, Terra Cotta Works, Leicestershire, 1918

Group of women terra cotta workers outside kiln, Leicestershire, 1918

Clay heap workers piling up the raw clay, Stoke-on-Trent, 1918

Clay being fed into mechanical tempering machine, Stoke-on-Trent, 1918

Furnace workers feeding coke to the furnaces in order to fire the pottery kilns, Stoke-on-Trent, 1918

Kiln workers loading a bottle kiln, Stoke-on-Trent, 1918. The kiln on the right has been sealed with bricks before firing

Kiln worker removing the shattered pots after firing, Stoke-on-Trent, 1918

Oven being emptied mechanically

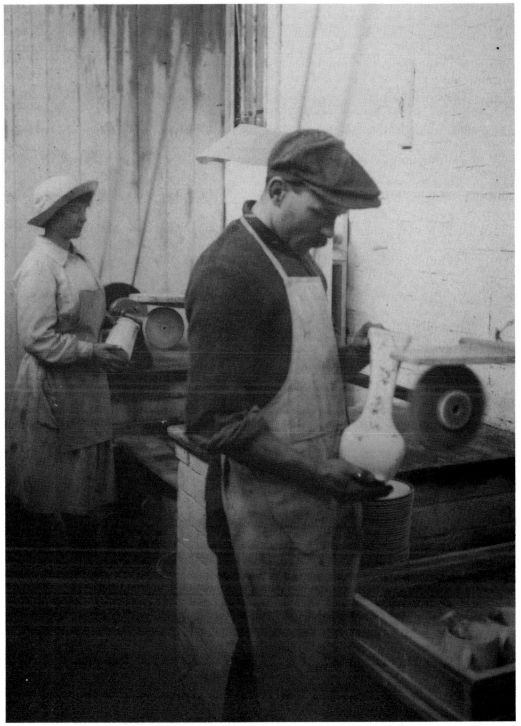

Pottery being finished by grinding down rough areas on an abrasive wheel, Stoke-on-Trent, 1918

Oven being emptied by hand, Stoke-on-Trent, 1918

Wash-house workers in Stoke-on-Trent pottery

Packing area in a pottery

Pottery medallions being moulded by hand

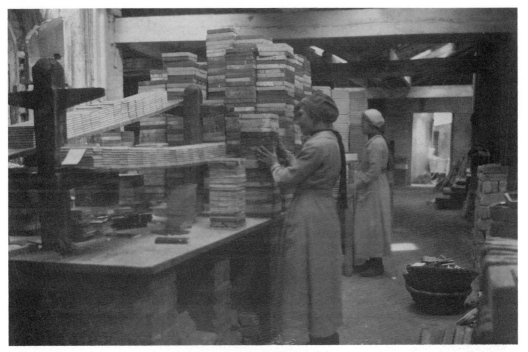

Tiles being checked after firing

Fine pottery being decorated by hand

LEATHER TRADES

During the war the number of women in the leather trades increased from 23,100 in July 1914 to 43,000 in 1918, the overwhelming majority of whom directly replaced men. Few women were employed in the heavy leather-tanning industry before the war, they were largely confined to the dry operations in the warehouses. By 1918 a third of the work-force in the tanning industry were female. Women employed in every area of work, both wet and dry, normally carrying out work which previously had been performed by youths. The Employers' Association at the end of the war assessed the performance of women, commenting on the high quality of their work, particularly in the areas requiring delicate handling and work which was of a repetitive nature. The employers noted that the women's timekeeping was better than the men's.

Some called it the compo shop, and others the knocking shop with a leering grin, the reason for this was that every girl was supplied with a large wooden mallet and a strong pair of scissors about ten to twelve inches long. These were her stock in trade without which she could not work, the mallets had an iron plate on the bottom and the shears were used to cut any thick skins.

The men started work at six a.m. and it was one of their tasks to wet the small skins, some of which were very small one never let your imagination run riot, this would be too horrible.

There was a huge vat filled with a boiling starchy liquid into which the bags of dried skins were emptied and allowed to pregnate for a period of time, they were then removed and drained on a huge slimey table from which they were weighed out. The girl would take the portion of slimey mess to her table on which was placed an iron frame, similar to a picture frame, measuring about twenty four inches by eighteen. There she would pick out the larger skins none of them more than four or five inches and stretch them on to the frame which stood on a hessian base. She would then proceed to fill in the centre of the frame with the pulpy mass left over, when this operation had been done she would take up the mallet and hammer the horrible mess until it was level and smooth, no holes left. Then she would turn in the edges of the layer on the bottom, the ends having been left over the rim of the frame in order to make a seal. This done she would proceed to place the skins left over on to the top of the layer of hammered pulp, this must be a neat operation otherwise the work was spoiled. The she would dash to the press which stood on the other side of the room and take up a square flat tin the same size as the sheet of work she had made, return to her table and transfer the whole thing on to the tray, place her number on the work rush over to the overlooker who could, if she so decided tear up the whole construction, or send you back to your table to patch it up. If you were lucky you would reach the 'old gals' table, this name was a sort of endearment, before anyone was there, and be rewarded for your work by a check which was the equivalent of one penny. These you stored in a tin and every morning at eleven a.m. you would join the queue to hand them into the office where the 'Old man' sat waiting. He entered the number of these checks into the book and the more you handed him the larger your pay on Friday evening. (Woman Leather Worker 1917)

Women tannery workers operating a 'setting out' machine, Nottingham, 1918

The tan-yard workers at the Pavlova Leather Company, Abingdon, 1918

CHEMICAL INDUSTRIES

Before World War I there were four times as many men than women employed in the fine chemical and drug industries, and very few in the heavy chemical industries. In all branches of the industry women were chiefly employed in the filling, labelling and finishing of packets or jars of chemicals or in the sorting and cleaning of bottles and jars. No women were employed in the Royal Gunpowder Factory before the war, a few women were employed at private explosive factories, mainly in the areas of teasing cotton, paste mixing for cordite, weighing and blending of cordite and making of blasting cartridges.

During the war the proportion of women working in the chemical industry rose from 20 per cent of the work-force to 39 per cent; the numbers of women increasing by sixty-four thousand, some thirty-four thousand of whom directly replaced men . The production of explosives absorbed the majority of these women, but the soap and candle industries also took in large numbers, an area where women had not worked before in significant numbers. In the heavy chemical industries, women were introduced during the war mainly as labourers, and were involved in packing, loading, unloading, trucking, wheeling and otherwise moving materials, and in general yard work. Depending upon the nature of the work, the Chemical Employers' Federation indicated that they considered that between 1.6 to 2.8 women were required to replace one man.

The Employers' Federation suggested that they were incurring additional costs by having to provide welfare supervisors, canteens, bath attendants, nurses, canteen staff, etc. for their women employees and these costs after the war would discourage them from employing large numbers of women.

The cork shed where the raw cork was stored in bales, Barry Ostlere and Shepherd Limited, Kirkcaldy, 1918

Cork-breaking area where the cork was ground, Barry Ostlere and Shepherd Limited, Kirkcaldy, 1918

The printing and coating machines for printing the designs on to the surface of the cork, Barry Ostlere and Shepherd Limited, Kirkcaldy, 1918

The packing floor, Barry Ostlere and Shepherd Limited, Kirkcaldy, 1918

Examining tables, Barry Ostlere and Shepherd Limited, Kirkcaldy, 1918

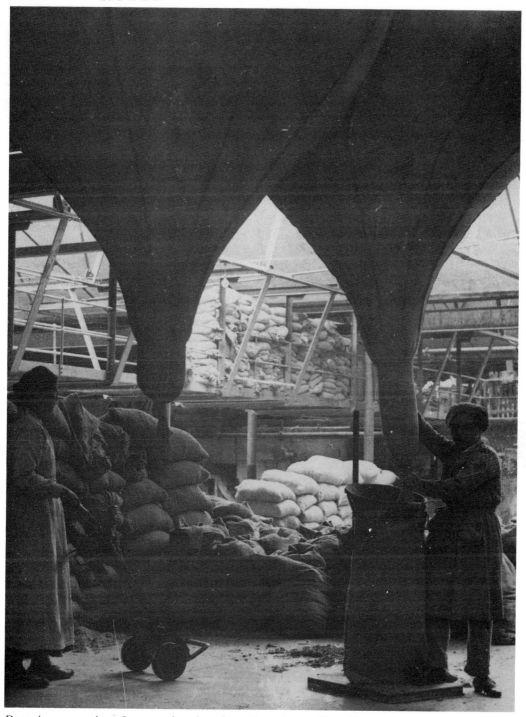

Dust-abstractor plant for removing dust from the asbestos fibre, Turner Brothers, Trafford Park, Manchester, 1918

Wheeling a bogey with wet asbestos millboard sheets to the drying room, Turner Brothers, Manchester, 1918

Dried asbestos sheeting being stacked, Turner Brothers, Manchester, 1918

Wet asbestos sheets being moulded into shape to form roofing sheets, Turner Brothers, Manchester, 1918

Asbestos roofing sheets being loaded on to railway wagons, Turner Brothers, Manchester, 1918

Corrugated asbestos sheeting being cut by guillotine, Turner Brothers, Manchester, 1918

Sewing asbestos mattresses for lining boilers on ships, Turner Brothers, Manchester, 1918

Asbestos mattresses being trucked to warehouse, Turner Brothers, Manchester, 1918

Asbestos cylinders for smoke shells being made by hand, Turner Brothers, Manchester, 1918

The treads on a rubber tyre being built up by hand

Stripping and hoisting tyres on frames for removal before applying the tread

Hoisting a tyre on a pulley for removal to the press

Fixing studded tread to a tyre

Trucking the raw rubber from the warehouse, Wood-Milne, Leyland, Lancashire

Raw rubber being warmed up and separated, Wood-Milne, Leyland, Lancashire

Raw rubber being warmed on a mill

Sheet rubber being prepared by being calendered, Wood-Milne, Leyland, Lancashire

Warm rubber being carried to the spreading room, Wood-Milne, Leyland, Lancashire

Woman rubber worker operating a spreading machine which coated canvas for tyre manufacture

Rubber inner tubes being made by hand

Rubber tubing being placed inside the vulcanisers

Calendering the rubber for producing a tread on a motor tyre. The tread was produced by running the soft rubber through the iron wheel in the background

Women glass workers separating the chard from glass. Note the poor protection for the hands when handling the razor-sharp raw glass pieces

Women sludge-pit workers

Sand being prepared for grinding

Plaster house workers. The plaster was used for bedding the glass on the surfacing tables

Trucking the glass composition to furnace
pots before firing

Holding the glass in position on the Lehr
tables

Women removing the glass from the Lehr table under the supervision of a male foreman

Glass being cleaned

Women carrying a sheet of glass from the Lehr table

Women removing used emery 'fells' which were used in polishing plate glass

Making wooden crates for rolled glass

Women operating glass-cutting machines with no protection to the face or hands

Woman engraving a glass bowl

Women finishing the bottoms of glass measuring jugs by grinding the bottoms smooth

Cutting off miners' lamp glasses

Thick glass for submarine portholes being packed.

PAPER AND PRINTING TRADES

The principal paper and printing trades in which women were employed before the war were printing, bookbinding, cardboard-box and paper making and paper-bag manufacture. The trade unions prevented women from preparing the machines or 'making ready' any job, although they could take the sheets of paper from the letter press. In Scotland, women were allowed to be involved in composition in the printing trade to a limited degree. In bookbinding, especially in the less skilled areas, women were employed on various stages of production such as paging, collating, folding and sewing. During the war the percentage of the total work-force employed by the paper and printing industries which were women rose from 36 per cent to 48 per cent, twenty-one thousand women directly replacing men. Married women were not discouraged from performing night work despite attempts by employers to relax the Factory and Workshop Acts, and replaced men mainly in warehouse work, bookbinding and paper making.

Warehouse where rags used in paper making were sorted

Women labourers feeding rags into the pulping machines

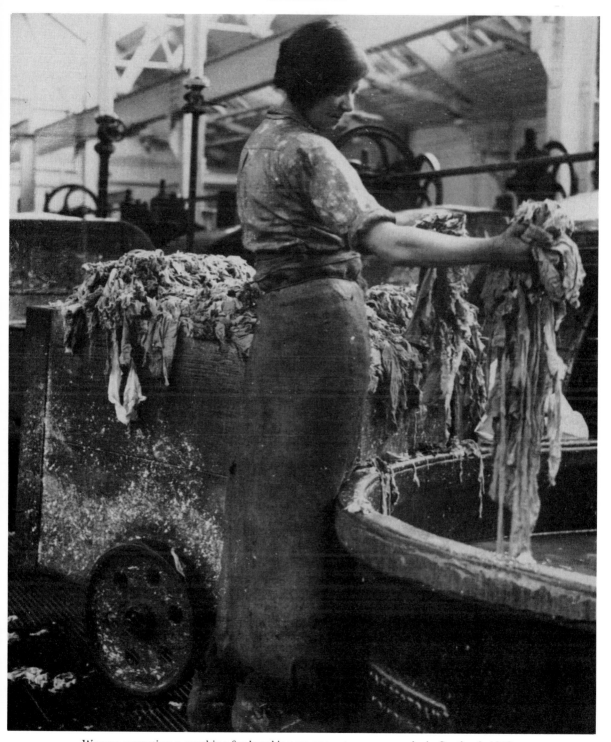

Woman operating a machine for breaking up rags at a paper works in Scotland, 1918

Woman trucking a load of boiled rags at a Scottish paper works

Woman worker preparing to feed a beating machine which prepares the pulp in the paper mill

Paper mills being fed pulp

Women operating a large industrial paper guillotine

Women checking the paper for quality before packing

The corrugating machine in a paper mill

Female yard workers unloading waste rolls of paper from a railway wagon

Bailing area for paper

Women compositors 'making ready' the letter presses

FOOD AND DRINK INDUSTRIES

Before 1914 women were confined to sack mending and light warehouse work in the grain-milling trade. In the larger bakeries, women were used to clean up and carry out light portering. In some biscuit factories they were employed on light-manufacturing operations such as icing, decorating biscuits by hand, chocolate dipping as well as the lining of tins with paper and packing by hand. No women were employed in the brewing and malting industries' central operations before the war, although some women were employed in the bottling departments on bottle washing, stacking and packing.

In these trades, between 1914–18, the percentage of women employed in the work-force rose from 35 per cent to 49 per cent, most of the increase due to women directly replacing men. The trades most affected were grain milling, bread and biscuit making and brewing. In the flour mills 7,800 women were introduced to men's work, being employed in such activities as sweeping, cleaning and packing, trucking and sack repair. There was vigorous opposition by the owners to the introduction of women and they only tolerated the use of women in the labour force due to the difficulties caused by the war. In brewing, women replaced thirteen thousand men filling casks (which was normally lads' work), weighing and breaking hops (men's work), cask and pulp washing, rinsing casks and testing. On light work it was reported by the brewers that a women in her twenties was regarded as being equal to a man; on heavy work three women were required to perform the work of two men. Often the companies introduced machinery to aid the heavy tasks, such as electric hoists to lift grain. In the bottling departments women were preferred to men and boys as they were considered to be more careful. Before the war no women were employed in the brewing or maltings processes, or in the office at Samuel Allsopp and Sons, Burton. Girls had been employed in the bottling department, on bottle washing, stacking, examining and packing. During the war the position changed completely: women were employed in all areas. A similar story was reported by Ind Coope: before the war no women or girls were employed in the breweries; during the war women were employed in brewing, maltings, bottling, stores, cooperages and offices.

Vat-house workers cleaning the lager store casks, Cheshire, 1918

Women brewery yard workers washing beer barrels for reuse, Cheshire, 1918

Beer barrels being re-hooped by women, London, 1918

Women coopers re-hooping and drilling the tap holes in beer barrels, London, 1918

Woman cooper re-hooping a barrel, London, 1918

TEXTILE AND CLOTHING INDUSTRIES

The textile trades were largely a women's industry before World War I, engaging two-fifths of all women who worked in industry, some four-fifths of the employees being female.

In the cotton industries the work of cleaning and loosening the cotton fibres was done by men, women were employed with men in the blowing and card room on machines laying the cotton fibres parallel. Spinning was done by men or women according to whether it was ring spinning or mule spinning. The majority of weavers were women working under the 'overlooking' of men. The weaver's work consisted almost entirely of keeping the shuttles furnished with cops of weft, placing the shuttles in the looms, replacing them by full ones as they became empty, repairing broken threads of the warp and stopping and starting the looms as the operators required. The number of looms worked by men was generally four, though in some districts they worked six with the assistance of a boy or girl known as a tenter. Women rarely worked more than four.

In the woollen and worsted trades the line of sex division was roughly the same as that of the cotton industry. As carried out in Yorkshire men performed mule spinning, women were employed exclusively on yarn reeling and winding. In wool-combing, men on night-shifts performed all the tasks normally carried out by women who were not permitted to carry out night-shift work. During the day, men were restricted to card-grinding and bowl-minding which were arduous, and wool drying which was extremely hot work.

During the war the proportion of women rose from 58 per cent to 67 per cent in the textile industry. The actual numbers of women did not rise overall; the areas of dyeing, hosiery and bleaching expanded considerably during the war due to the requirements of the Army and Navy and absorbed large numbers of women; however, the period was also one which saw considerable shrinkage in the cotton industry. By 1918, there was a substitution of men by women of around sixty thousand within the industry. During the war, women replaced men by working on frame-machines, knitting-machines, and in pressing, boarding, stockroom and warehouse. Handknitting-machines which before the war were considered too heavy for women were now operated by them. The work produced by the women was assessed as being equivalent to that of men's; despite this the Employers' Federation were determined that pre-war division of labour would be revived and married women sent home.

The warping machine, Nottingham, 1918

Replacing empty spools, Nottingham, 1918

Threading the bobbins, Nottingham, 1918

Putting up a warp, Nottingham, 1918

Putting up a thread on a lace-curtain machine, Nottingham, 1918

Changing the jacquard cards on a Platferns
alcove lace machine, Nottingham, 1918

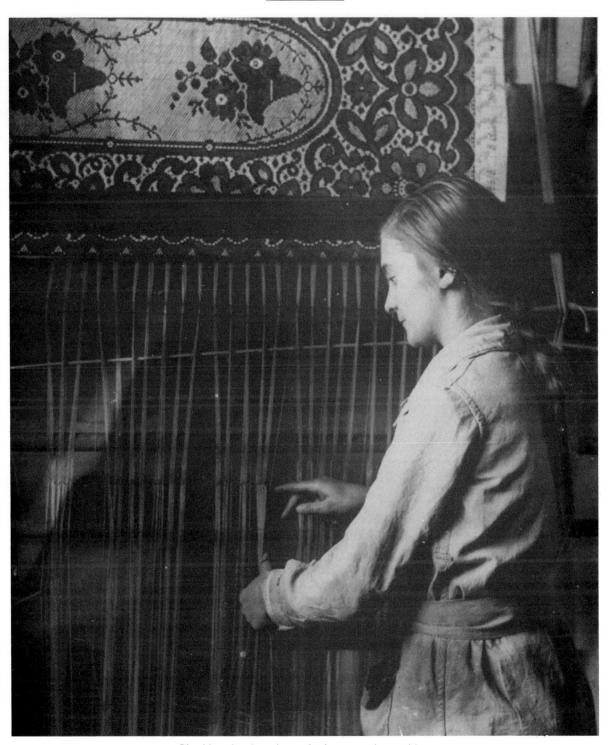

Checking the threads on the lace-curtain machine

The mending room in a Nottingham-lace factory. Natural light only was being used and so all the machines are arranged around the side of the room by the windows

Lace workers with their teacher, Nottingham, 1918

Finished lace articles

Women loading the yarn on to a barrow

Women workers attending the frames where the individual yarns form strands

A stranding machine for producing house rope

Women rope workers in a rope walk 170 fathom in length

Packing rope for the Navy

Baling the jute

The warping machines, Weldon and Wilkinson, New Basford, Nottingham

Women trimming stockings

Women trimming army socks, Weldon and Wilkinson, New Basford, Nottingham

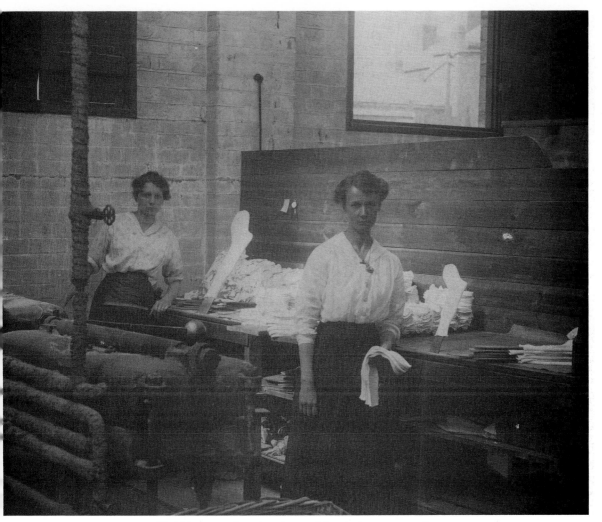

Finishing area for trimming and inspecting army socks

Warehouse workers in a wool-sorting area

Drying area for wool

Carding machine in a wool factory

SELECTED BIBLIOGRAPHY

Andrews, I.O.   *The Economic Effects of the World War upon Women and Children in Great Britain.* Second edition, Oxford University Press, 1921.
Bell, Lady F.   *At the Works.* London, 1907.
Black, C. (ed.)   *Married Women's Work.* London, 1915.
Booth, C.   *Life and Labour of the People of London, 1890–1911.*
Braybon, G.   *Women Workers in the First World War.* Routledge, 1989.
Burnett, J.   *Useful Toil.* Allen Lane, 1974.
Drake, B.   *Women in the Engineering Trades.* Fabian Research Paper, London, 1917.
Pankhurst, E.S.   *The Home Front.* Hutchinson, London, 1932.
Pennington, S. and
   Westover, B. (eds)   *A Hidden Workforce: Homeworkers in England, 1850–1985.* Macmillan, 1989.
Stone, G. (ed.)   *Women War Workers.* London, 1917.

Government Papers

Health and Safety Inspectorate Annual Reports, 1913–1920.
War Cabinet Committee on Women in Industry, 1919. Cmd. 135 & 167.
Report of the Women's Advisory Committee on the Domestic Service Problem, 1919. Cmd. 67.

INDEX